THE POETRY OF PLATINUM

The Poetry of Platinum

Walter the Educator

Silent King Books

SILENT KING BOOKS

SKB

Copyright © 2024 by Walter the Educator

All rights reserved. No part of this book may be reproduced in any manner whatsoever without written permission except in the case of brief quotations embodied in critical articles and reviews.

First Printing, 2024

Disclaimer
This book is a literary work; poems are not about specific persons, locations, situations, and/or circumstances unless mentioned in a historical context. This book is for entertainment and informational purposes only. The author and publisher offer this information without warranties expressed or implied. No matter the grounds, neither the author nor the publisher will be accountable for any losses, injuries, or other damages caused by the reader's use of this book. The use of this book acknowledges an understanding and acceptance of this disclaimer.

"Earning a degree in chemistry changed my life!"
- Walter the Educator

dedicated to all the chemistry lovers, like myself, across the world

Where elements dance their ballet,

PLATINUM

A noble metal shimmers bright and gay,

PLATINUM

Platinum, the sovereign of lustrous array,

PLATINUM

In its essence, a story we fervently portray.

PLATINUM

From Earth's hidden vaults, where shadows dwell,

PLATINUM

Platinum emerges, a silent spell,

PLATINUM

Forged in cosmic fires, where mysteries swell,

PLATINUM

Its genesis, a saga no tongue can tell.

PLATINUM

In the alchemy of stars, where fusion thrives,

PLATINUM

Platinum seeds bloom, where the cosmos derives,

PLATINUM

Its atoms intertwined, in celestial hives,

PLATINUM

A testament to the universe's creative dives.

PLATINUM

Upon Earth's crust, in rivers and in veins,

PLATINUM

Platinum lies dormant, where silence reigns,

PLATINUM

Yet beneath its stoic facade, life sustains,

PLATINUM

In its depths, the promise of wealth and gains.

PLATINUM

O noble Platinum, in thy atomic core,

PLATINUM

Lies the secrets of ages, forevermore,

PLATINUM

A guardian of dreams, on wisdom's shore,

PLATINUM

In thy radiant grace, we humbly adore.

PLATINUM

In the hands of artisans, thy form transforms,

PLATINUM

Crafted into wonders, where beauty norms,

PLATINUM

From crowns of kings to humble charms,

PLATINUM

Thy allure enchants, in myriad swarms.

PLATINUM

In the crucible of science, thy wonders unfold,

PLATINUM

A catalyst for change, in discoveries bold,

PLATINUM

From laboratories to industries cold,

PLATINUM

Thy utility reigns, a fortune untold.

PLATINUM

But beyond thy material worth, thy virtues shine,

PLATINUM

As a symbol of endurance, in the grand design,

PLATINUM

Thou art a beacon of hope, in the darkest brine,

PLATINUM

Guiding humanity, with a light divine.

PLATINUM

For in thy resilience, we find our resolve,

PLATINUM

To weather the storms, and problems solve,

PLATINUM

In thy noble essence, we dare to evolve,

PLATINUM

Towards a future where dreams absolve.

PLATINUM

O Platinum, in thy mystical allure,

PLATINUM

We find reflections of our essence pure,

PLATINUM

In thy journey, we see our own obscure,

PLATINUM

A quest for meaning, forever to endure.

PLATINUM

So let us sing praises to Platinum's grace,

PLATINUM

In its gleaming visage, we find solace,

PLATINUM

A symbol of resilience, in life's race,

PLATINUM

An emblem of hope, in every place.

PLATINUM

ABOUT THE CREATOR

Walter the Educator is one of the pseudonyms for Walter Anderson. Formally educated in Chemistry, Business, and Education, he is an educator, an author, a diverse entrepreneur, and he is the son of a disabled war veteran. "Walter the Educator" shares his time between educating and creating. He holds interests and owns several creative projects that entertain, enlighten, enhance, and educate, hoping to inspire and motivate you.

Follow, find new works, and stay up to date
with Walter the Educator™
at WaltertheEducator.com

www.ingramcontent.com/pod-product-compliance
Lightning Source LLC
LaVergne TN
LVHW052007060526
838201LV00059B/3885